BROKEN *and* UNASHAMED

Pieced Together by the Love of God

Terri-Ann Marie Nelson

WESTBOW
PRESS®
A DIVISION OF THOMAS NELSON
& ZONDERVAN

WestBow Press books may be ordered through booksellers or by contacting:

WestBow Press
A Division of Thomas Nelson & Zondervan
1663 Liberty Drive
Bloomington, IN 47403
www.westbowpress.com
1 (866) 928-1240

Because of the dynamic nature of the Internet, any web addresses or
links contained in this book may have changed since publication and
may no longer be valid. The views expressed in this work are solely those
of the author and do not necessarily reflect the views of the publisher,
and the publisher hereby disclaims any responsibility for them.

Any people depicted in stock imagery provided by Thinkstock are models,
and such images are being used for illustrative purposes only.
Certain stock imagery © Thinkstock.

ISBN: 978-1-5127-7913-4 (sc)
ISBN: 978-1-5127-7914-1 (e)

Library of Congress Control Number: 2017903974

Print information available on the last page.

WestBow Press rev. date: 3/21/2017

*This book is dedicated to the beautiful young ladies I have had
the privilege of serving who has entrusted me with their stories.
Whose stories have encouraged me to write my
own in hopes of revealing how real God is.
In them I am reminded of the grace of God
and what He has purposed me for.
This book is for all who have been broken who I hope will
allow God's love to piece them back together again.*

CONTENTS

ACKNOWLEDGEMENTS

I never imagined putting to print my story. As a matter of a fact, I laughed when the idea was suggested. You see, my personal story of abuse was one I believed I would take to the grave with me. But that's the thing about purpose. God has a way of taking you from where you are comfortable and stretching you beyond what you could ever imagine for your life. That's the sacrifice of saying yes to God's will and way for your life. You are allowing him to use all of you – even those things that once brought you pain to bring him glory. This process of not only writing but publishing a book has been an interesting one to say the least. And would not have happened without special people in my life. People that I am truly blessed to call my family and friends. And so, I would like to take a moment and just say thank you.

A special thank you to my mother Janet Mair, who continues to support my every endeavor and continues to be my biggest fan Without you mother, I would not be the woman I am

A special thank you to my pastor, Bishop Devon Dixon, who continues to challenge me to live a life of purpose Thank you for taking the time to read my manuscript and being a part of this project

A special thank you to my dear friend Riley Gray, who is the definition and embodiment of a Godly friend/sister Thank you for all your prayers and words of encouragement Oh and thank you for your moments of ratchetness that keeps me laughing

A special thank you to my friend Kaydine Bent, who volunteered her time to read and even cry throughout this book

A special thank you to The PULSE Young Adult Board and honorary member: Tisha, Janna, Lesa, and Samantha, and Sara – you ladies are the type of friends people dream of having Thank you for your hugs, support, messages, and laughs

And a special thank you to you, the reader for picking up this book and allowing it to be a blessing in your life

FOREWORD

Terri-Ann Marie Nelson, a former abuse victim, brings openness to the subject of abuse. A subject that is often too difficult to discuss by those who are victims themselves. Although, abuse is a topic so familiar in the church community it is seldom addressed.

This is a book about empowerment. It is about giving a voice to victims of sexual abuse. It is about turning victims to victors; turning pain into praise; moving from shame to glory. It's about recovery, redemption and about finding freedom after abuse.

I believe the author makes a powerful case for this book when she says, "the devil attempted to isolate us due to our abuse, where we felt too ashamed to speak out. But now we are giving our pain a voice and turning it into a song of praise. Therefore, when one of us turns from being victim to being a victor, then we all win and celebrate together."

The author takes us on an honest journey of how she worked through her own pain by recognizing the abuse and the damage done. The road she travelled was one marked by betrayal in love and by broken trust. She shares her many failed attempts to sedate her pain by looking for love in all the wrong places until Jesus met her at the intersection of the brokenness and pain. There He revealed his love for her and taught her how to overcome the damage she suffered more appropriately.

This book reveals how the redemptive love of God and the power of forgiveness can bring victims out of isolation and into the marvelous light of the gospel. It is a must read for both those who ever suffered from abuse, or for those who seek to help someone overcome abuse. Again, in her own powerful words, "…when one of us turns from being victim to being victor, then we all win and celebrate together.

I believe many lives will have cause to celebrate again simply by reading this book.

~ Pastor Devon Dixon

OPENING REMARKS

First, I would like to thank God for giving me the confidence to put my story in ink and share my testimony with you. I am beyond humbled that he has chosen me to be a vessel that will pour his words into you, those who are broken and in need of love. I am thankful that he has not only healed me, but also made me whole, and I pray the same for you.

I also would like to thank you for picking up this book. Maybe you purposely sought it out for yourself or for someone else, or maybe you just stumbled across it and found yourself curious. Whatever the reason, I truly believe God led you to my story, and I pray that it blesses you in ways you never imagined. And please pass it along, because you never know who else might benefit from it.

Finally, I want to thank those friends with whom God has blessed me, who inspired me to share my story and write this book. Thank you to those who encouraged me and helped me along this journey. Your words of encouragement, your suggestions, and your late-night edits have been greatly appreciated.

Now that that's out of the way, I pray you are blessed beyond anything I could ever hope for or imagine.

Quick disclosure! Throughout the book, you will notice that I use first-person pronouns such as *we* and *us*. Why? Because our brokenness is something we have in common and we are going on this healing journey together. The Devil tries to isolate us when we feel too ashamed to speak out because of our abuse. But now we are giving our pain a voice and turning it into a song of praise. When one of us turns from being a victim to being a victor, we all win and celebrate together.

The journey to healing will look different for each person, but it always begins with recognition of the abuse and the damage it has done. Healing continues as we learn to trust Jesus and release all our pain to him. The road is long and may require safe companions, such as a counselor, a pastor, and loving family members. But trust me when I say that you are not alone on this journey!

1

HELLO THERE

Well, hello there! As you read this book, imagine you and me sitting down together with delicious plates of food. (I love food!) Over this delicious meal, I will share my story with you. It's a story that begins with me being sexually abused as a child, but thankfully it does not end there. The story turns into a journey of being lost and then being found by God. The journey on which God takes me is one of healing and wholeness. And now, God and I invite you to start your own journey.

Because I never spoke about it, I became numb to the pain and as a result, I figured, I was emotionally okay. I no longer dwelled on what happened. Instead, I placed the sexual abuse and everything associated with it into a box and buried it deep down somewhere. Then I covered this box with alcohol, sex, school, and work, so that it was impossible to open—or at least would require a huge amount of effort to do so. And trust me, I had no plan to expose, deal with, or share my secret.

But even though I chose not to think about the abuse, the past was definitely creeping into the present—and I had no idea how it would affect my future. For obvious and understandable reasons, I had trust issues and relationship problems. I did not believe in love.

Physically I was fine, and intellectually I was at the top of my class, but I was broken emotionally.

I was convinced I would spend the rest of my life alone. Why? Well, because of the abuse I had experienced, I had learned to hate myself. Every time I looked into the mirror, I was disgusted with what I saw. I believed that if anyone learned what had happened to me, they would be disgusted as well. And who could ever possibly love me? I believed I was unworthy of love. But boy, I'm so glad that I was completely wrong. I *am* worth loving—and so are you.

Somewhere, sometime, someone hurt you and attempted to break you. This person stole all your joy and peace, leaving you in pieces. You were lost, trying desperately to find your way out but to no avail. Love? What is that? Love is what betrayed you, after all.

I have been where you are. I sat there with a smile on my face, pretending everything was fine, but on the inside I was slowly dying. Maybe like you, I actually considered taking my own life. In fact, one day I almost did.

I stood at the kitchen sink, knife in hand, and heard a voice—a voice that promised me things would get better. Either I was crazy and hearing voices, or God was reassuring me that this pain shall surely pass. Those words were enough reason for me to choose to live another day. That should be enough reason for you to choose to live another day as well.

I grew up in the church and was saved at a young age, but I did not completely surrender to God until I was a young adult. I was lost in the pew and found myself in the world. I was attempting to self-heal and cover the wounds of my past by self-medicating with alcohol and bandaging my bruises with the validations of boys. I was searching for happiness, worth, and love in dark places.

Maybe you are searching for those things in dark places, too. Maybe that's why you keep bumping into the wrong people, attracting the wrong men, and stumbling over sex, drugs, alcohol, and lies.

You're in need of a light to help illuminate your way out. That light is Jesus Christ! That light found me in my dark corner and revealed to me what love really is. That light healed me and made me whole. That light gave me a purpose and the confidence to write this book.

This book is for all those who have been betrayed by love and broken by trust. This book is for those who have attempted to piece themselves together, and for those who are an inch away from giving up. This book is for those who are in desperate need of a Savior.

Prayer

Lord, thank you for the lives of the people who are reading this book. Lord, you know their stories and exactly what they have been through. God, you have seen every tear that has fallen, and you have heard the cries of their hearts.

But God, I declare the chains that have been holding them in bondage to their pasts will be broken in Jesus's name. I declare that they will no longer view themselves as victims but as the victors you have called them to be. Lord, let them know they are not alone and that you are there with them, even right now. Help them understand that even when they felt abandoned by you, you were right there with them.

Lord, comfort them right now, and may the words in this book inspire them to seek you. May this book encourage them to pursue an authentic relationship with you. Lord, help them understand that there is no pain in vain, and that you are working out all things for their good.

In Jesus' name I pray, Amen.

2

WHY ME?

For those who love God, all things
work together for good,
for those who are called according to his purpose.
—**Romans 8:28 (ESV)**

Why me? That is the million-dollar question. I'm sure you've asked God, time and time again, "Why me?" And most likely you provided your own incorrect answers. Maybe you told yourself that you were being punished for something, or that God obviously does not love you or care what happens to you. It's understandable that you might feel that way.

I used to share those same sentiments, but now I hope to persuade you to abandon those incorrect thoughts. Through the pages of this book, I want to challenge you to learn just how much God truly cares for you.

Below are two verses that remind me how much I mean to God. The first one reminds me that God has not forgotten me. If something with little value like a sparrow is not forgotten by God then I, who means so much to him that he knows how many strands of hair are on my head, am not forgotten by him either. And the last one reminds me of how special I am to God. God is involved in my life from the very beginning. And by beginning I mean from conception. And from conception I am special because God knitted and intricately put me together.

Anything made intricately means that the creator is taking their time crafting their masterpiece. They pay attention to every single detail and when they are finished they are proud of what they created. Therefore, I am fearfully, wonderfully, and beautifully made since it is God who created me. And so are you!

"Are not five sparrows sold for two pennies? Yet not one of them is forgotten by God. Indeed, the very hairs of your head are all numbered. Don't be afraid; you are worth more than many sparrows" (Luke 12:6–7 NIV).

"For you formed my inward parts; you knitted me together in my mother's womb. I praise you, for I am fearfully and wonderfully made. Wonderful are your works; my soul knows it very well. My frame was not hidden from you, when I was being made in secret, intricately woven in the depths of the earth" (Psalm 139: 13-15 ESV).

And Then There Was Sin

Before we tackle the "Why me?" question, we first need to understand "Why?" Why does such evil as abuse, pain, and hurt even exist? Evil in the world can be traced to the beginning of time in the garden of Eden, when Eve was tricked by the serpent into doing the one act that God had commanded Adam not to do.

> Now the serpent was more crafty than any of the wild animals the Lord God had made. He said to the woman, "Did God really say, 'You must not eat from any tree in the garden'?" The woman said to the serpent, "We may eat fruit from the trees in the garden, but God did say, 'You must not eat fruit from the tree that is in the middle of the garden,

and you must not touch it, or you will die.'" ...
When the woman saw that the fruit of the tree
was good for food and pleasing to the eye, and also
desirable for gaining wisdom, she took some and ate
it. She also gave some to her husband, who was with
her, and he ate it. (Genesis 3:1–3, 6 NIV)

God had allowed Adam to eat of any tree in the garden except
one, and it was this forbidden tree from which the crafty serpent
tempted Eve to eat. Not only did Eve eat from this tree, but she also
shared the fruit with her husband. Adam broke the one command
God had given him, and because of Adam's disobedience, sin entered
the world: "When Adam sinned, sin entered the world. Adam's sin
brought death, so death spread to everyone, for everyone sinned"
(Romans 5:12 NLT).

Evil, destruction, suffering, and difficulties are a result of Adam's
disobedience. Because of sin, people have become evil, which causes
them to inflict pain, hurt, and abuse on others. Unfortunate? Yes.
Thankfully, a day will come when there will be no more evil, and
everything that is wrong with the world will be made right:

God is just: He will pay back trouble to those who
trouble you and give relief to you who are troubled,
and to us as well. This will happen when the Lord
Jesus is revealed from heaven in blazing fire with
his powerful angels. He will punish those who do
not know God and do not obey the gospel of our
Lord Jesus. They will be punished with everlasting
destruction and shut out from the presence of the
Lord and from the glory of his might on the day
he comes to be glorified in his holy people and to
be marveled at among all those who have believed.
This includes you. (2 Thessalonians 1:6–10a NIV)

A Powerful God?

Now that we understand why there is evil in the world, let's approach another "Why?" question. Why doesn't God stop evil from happening? He is all-powerful, so he is capable of intervening if he really wants to, right? "The Bible tells us that God is holy (Isaiah 6:3), righteous (Psalm 7:11), just (Deuteronomy 32:4), and sovereign (Daniel 4:17–25)."[1] I know, these characteristics don't make sense when applied to a God who allowed us to be abused. In fact, those characteristics "tell us the following about God: (1) God can prevent evil, and (2) God desires to rid the universe of evil. So, if both are true, then why does God allow evil?"[2]

The answer is simple—maybe too simple—but it all boils down to free will. God created us as human beings who can think and make decisions freely of our own will. God did not design us to be robots or puppets that he can control. Because God could have "programmed" us to be perfect, only doing what is right and pleasing in his sight. But then there would not be any meaningful relationships between him and us. And that is what God desires—a meaningful relationship between him, the creator, and mankind, his creation. God is a gentleman. He will not force himself upon us; instead, he allows us to choose whether we want to be with him.

A Call to Worship

God created us to worship him, but worship is our choice. We decide whether we want to pursue a genuine relationship with him. We choose whether we want to live according to his will and his way. We have free will.

God's first human creation, Adam and Eve, were innocently enjoying a world without sin, He allowed them to live in his presence in the Garden of Eden with only one command – not to eat the

---

[1] "Why Does God Allow Evil?"
[2] "Why Does God Allow Evil?"

fruit from the tree of knowledge of good and evil. God gave Adam and Eve the choice of either listening and obeying or ignoring and rejecting his command. Because of this free will, Adam and Eve could either respond to God's love by trusting him or they could choose to disobey. Unfortunately, they chose to disobey.[3] And Adam's choice to disobey God caused the world to live under the curse of sin. We face a similar choice—either trust God or live life our own way.

I'll admit that I tried to live life my own way, and I made a huge mess of things. But I learned that trying to be in control of my own life is impossible and, may I add, quite stressful. I needed to relinquish control to someone greater, to someone who created the whole world, to someone who designed me as a unique person and knows the plans he has for me.

"My frame was not hidden from you when I was made in the secret place, when I was woven together in the depths of the earth. Your eyes saw my unformed body; all the days ordained for me were written in your book" (Psalm 139:15–16 NIV).

"Before I formed you in the womb I knew you, before you were born I set you apart" (Jeremiah 1:5 NIV).

"'For I know the plans I have for you,' declares the Lord, 'plans to prosper you and not to harm you, plans to give you a hope and a future'" (Jeremiah 29:11 NIV).

The way I see it, God is a father who wants only what is best for his children. God wants us to succeed and live purposeful lives. God does not want us to fail or endure constant abuse or suffering. By giving my life to God, I admitted that I could not do this thing called *life* without him. I admitted that I desperately needed him. I admitted that I desperately needed his love, healing, guidance, and direction. And since I surrendered my life to Christ, he has never failed me.

By turning my life over to God, I have gained a genuine

---

[3] "Why Does God Allow Evil?"

happiness independent of others' opinions and validations. I no longer need to be popular on social media or go out partying every weekend. Nor do I need to find love in the arms of a man. All I need is God's approval. I have also experienced an amazing peace. No matter what troubling situation I am going through, I know I will be okay, because God has me. I say all this to encourage you to pursue an authentic and genuine relationship with God. "And the peace of God, which transcends all understanding, will guard your hearts and your minds in Christ Jesus" (Philippians 4:7 NIV).

God created a real world where we, just like Adam and Eve, can choose between good and evil. Their decision to do wrong ended up hurting us—and will continue to hurt us unless we decide to deal with the pain in a more appropriate and correct way. More on this later.

So, could God have intervened and prevented my abuse? Yes, "God is perfectly capable of intervening supernaturally 100 percent of the time."[4] Why doesn't he? Because God would then be forced to intervene in every other area of our lives as well. God would have to prevent us from telling a lie, cheating on a test, drinking or smoking, entering a relationship that seemed—but actually wasn't—good for us, or anything else we do that is not godly. Although a perfect God created us, sin entered the world, causing us to be flawed and separating us from him.

Despite our flaws and sinful nature, God made a way to reconnect with us, by sending his son, Jesus Christ, to die for us. Our sins were crucified on the cross. Jesus left the comforts of heaven to come down to earth to die. Why? Because God believes we are worth dying for. Why? Because we are his creation and he desires a relationship with us. Why? Because God desires all of us to willingly choose to obey and pursue him. Why? Because God loves us unconditionally.

And when we decide to have a relationship with God and follow

---

[4] "Why Does God Allow Evil?"

his way, God promises that things will go well, not only for us but also for our children, and our children's children, and ... Well, you get the picture. "Oh that they had such a heart as this always, to fear me and to keep all my commandments, that it might go well with them and with their descendants forever!" (Deuteronomy 5:29 ESV).

When we choose to do things our own way, we tend to blame God for not doing anything about it when things go wrong. Such is the heart of a sinful man. But God, in all his wisdom and glory, sent his son, Jesus, to change the hearts of those who choose to turn from evil. If we will call on Jesus, he will save us from their sin and its consequences.

Unfortunately, many people refuse to be transformed and continue to live life their way, not caring how their evil deeds affect others. As a result, we all suffer the consequences of their evil. But rather than blame God and ask why he does not prevent *all* evil, we should be about the business of proclaiming the cure for evil and its consequences—Jesus Christ! "Declare his glory among the nations, his wonder among all peoples" (Psalm 96:3 NKJV).

So Why Me?

Now, let's get back to the "Why me?" question. Unfortunately, I cannot answer this question for you. I cannot understand or even try to attempt to understand the inner workings of the mind of someone who finds pleasure in abusing someone else. But I can tell you this—God does *not* use abuse as punishment, and he *does* love you. In fact, Psalm 34:18 (NIV) tells us, "The Lord is close to the brokenhearted and saves those who are crushed in spirit."

God is close to those who are broken and suffer pain, and he is ready to heal those who ask for his help. He is willing to reveal those areas of your life that you are desperately hiding and avoiding. He is ready to heal and restore you from the inside out.

I challenge you to change "Why me?" into "Why *not* me?" God is not the author of our pain, but he can use our pain for his purpose in our lives. In other words, God does not cause people to sin, and he did not cause someone to abuse you. But he can use that abuse and your subsequent pain and suffering for his glory.

Someone else might not have survived what you went through, but you did. And because you lived through it, you can speak to it. Because I have experienced, survived, and been healed from my abuse, I can now speak to other victims of abuse. And because we have survived our abuse, we are now graduates with a testimony. "For those who love God, all things work together for good, for those who are called according to his purpose" (Romans 8:28 ESV).

I truly believe that when God has something great planned for your life, the Devil will stop at nothing to make sure God's plans never come to fruition. The Devil used those people close to me to abuse me, and that abuse left me emotionally scarred. As I became uncomfortable in my own skin, my scars lowered my self-esteem, resulting in a loss of confidence. As long as I remained angry with God, the Devil was winning. As long as I turned to alcohol and sex, rather than to God, the Devil was winning. The Devil was winning as long as God was unable to use me.

But oh, how the tables have turned! When I personally acknowledged the abuse for what it was—*abuse*—the truth set me free. And it is that freedom that broke the chains the Devil was using to keep me hostage. God is now taking my story and turning my pain into a song of praise. Now I can sing, "Why *not* me?"

"Why not me?" is my Job moment. After Job lost everything—and I do mean everything—everyone wanted him to curse God and just die. "His wife said to him, 'You are still as faithful as ever, aren't you? Why don't you curse God and die?'" (Job 2:9 GNTD).

But Job, knowing who God is and how great God is, refused. Job was essentially telling the Devil, "Give me your best shot. But no matter what, I will continue to praise God." "Job answered, 'You are talking nonsense! When God sends us something good, we welcome it. How can we complain when he sends us trouble?' Even in all the suffering, Job said nothing against God" (Job 2:10 GNTD).

"[Job] said, 'I was born with nothing, and I will die with nothing. The Lord gave, and now he has taken away. May his name be praised!' In spite of everything that had happened, Job did not sin by blaming God" (Job 1:21–22 GNTD).

I'm basically telling the Devil to do what he wants to me. But I'm also putting him on notice that no matter what he does, I will continue to praise God, because I know and understand who God is and how great he is.

God wants you to know who he is and how great he is. He wants you to understand that your pain has not been in vain, and he would love for you to realize the testimony that you now have. God wants to wash away your past and shower you with his love, joy, and peace.

Your abuse is not the end of your story—it is just one chapter, or maybe even the beginning of a beautiful love story between you and God. There is a reason why you survived your abuse. There is a purpose for your pain. For me, my abuse has allowed me to connect with women who have similar stories and empathize with them. My abuse is a tool that God is using to show what healing, wholeness, and victory look like. God is using my abuse to encourage you and let you know that it is possible to trust and love again. My abuse is an example of God working out all things for my good.

"But, indeed for this reason I have allowed you to remain, in order to show you my power and in order to proclaim my name through all the earth" (Exodus 9:16 NASB). What is the reason for your pain? You now have a choice to make—allow the Devil to win by remaining hurt and bitter, or give all your pain to God and allow him to heal you.

Prayer

Lord, I don't want the Devil to win any longer, and so I give you all my pain. Lord, heal me physically and emotionally. Erase the scars from my heart, so that I am no longer hurt and bitter.

Help me, God, to understand that no pain is in vain. Reveal to me who you are, even in times of darkness. Thank you for my testimony, which you will use to give you all the glory.

Amen.

3

WHERE ARE YOU?

*But to you I have cried out, O Lord, and in the
morning my prayer comes before you. Lord, why do you
cast off my soul? Why do you hide your face from me?
I have been afflicted and ready to die from my youth; I
suffer your terrors; I am distraught. Your fierce wrath
has gone over me; your terrors have cut me off. They
came around me all day long like water; they engulfed
me altogether. Loved one and friend you have put
far from me, and my acquaintances into darkness.*
—Psalm 88:13–18 (NKJV)

I never felt more alone than when the reality of my abuse hit
me. When I came to terms with what had happened to me, I felt
disgusted and isolated, and I believed no one would understand.
Despite attending and being active in church, turning to God
seemed ridiculous. I figured that what had happened to me was
either (1) too big for God to handle or (2) too small for him to care
about, especially when compared with everything else going on in
the world. As I now know, I was completely wrong.

Gigantic Fears

No problem is too big for God to handle. When we believe that our hurts, pains, and abuse are too big for God to take care of, we are limiting a limitless God. We are telling God, "Yes, you are powerful enough to cause the blind to see, the deaf to hear, and the sick to be healed. But you are not powerful enough to fix me." Doesn't make sense, does it? By focusing on our problems, rather than on the problem solver, we invite fear to live in our hearts.

In the Old Testament, God made a promise that his people would live in "a land flowing with milk and honey." As the story goes, God's people, the Israelites, spent time wandering in the wilderness. Meanwhile God was proving to his people, time and time again, how powerful he was. He freed the Israelites from slavery and led them out of Egypt. He parted the Red Sea for them to cross, and then allowed the waters to return and destroy the mighty Egyptian army. He fought on behalf of the Israelites, allowing them to conquer great nations. And now the time had come for them to enter the land that God had promised to them.

Moses sent twelve men to spy out the land, and they came back and reported that the land was indeed fruitful and flowing with milk and honey. But there was one problem, one gigantic problem. The land was inhabited by giants.

What do you do when faced with a gigantic problem? Are you like ten of the spies, who said, "We are not able to go up against the people, for they are stronger than we [are] … There we saw the giants; and we were like grasshoppers in our own sight, and so we were in their sight" (Numbers 13:31, 33 NKJV)? Do you believe what you are going through is an insurmountable obstacle that God is unable to overcome? Are you allowing fear to rule in your heart?

Or are you going to be like the other two spies, Joshua and Caleb, who said, "Let us go up at once and take possession, for we are well able to overcome it" (Numbers 13:30 NKJV)? Do you believe that our God is bigger than the gigantic pain of our abuse?

Problems, like giants, are able to hold you captive only as long as you let them. The more you think and talk about them, or avoid talking about them, the bigger they will become in your mind. You might think that your problem is the physical, sexual, or emotional abuse that you endured, but the real problem is your perspective. When you focus more on the abuse you are saying that thing you went through is too big or too powerful to ever get over. You are saying there is no way you will ever move past the abuse. And being unable to move past the abuse will cause you to live a life of pain.

Living a life of pain cripples you! You have allowed yourself to become comfortable in your pain. Your outlook on life is dim because your expectations are low. Because of the pain you begin to believe that you do not deserve the best and you begin to settle for a life of mediocrity. Living a life of pain causes you to hurt people because as the saying goes, "hurt people hurt people." So how do you break free from a life of pain? You look to God!

The more you focus on how much bigger God is, the easier it will be for you to prevail over your giants. When you tell your pain, hurt, and abuse that they are nothing compared to a powerful and great God, they have no other choice but to cower in defeat. Do not be afraid to deal with your pain. After all, God did not give us the spirit of fear: "For God has not given us a spirit of fear and timidity, but of power, love, and self-discipline" (2 Timothy 1:7 NLT). You have a choice to make – choose to either focus on the abuse or choose to focus on God.

Joshua and Caleb had confidence that the God they served would be able to do what seemed impossible. They were confident because they believed God's promise that the land belonged to them, and they witnessed the works of God's hands.

In Exodus 15:26, God declares, "I am the Lord who heals you." God is Jehovah Rapha, the Lord who heals you, and he promises to heal us of all hatred, hurt, resentfulness, bitterness, and brokenness if we allow him to enter our hearts. Will you have confidence in his promise to heal?

A Caring God

God cares about every minute detail of our lives. "Now if God so clothes the grass of the field, which today is, and tomorrow is thrown into the oven, will he not much more clothe you? ... Therefore do not worry" (Matthew 6:30–31 NKJV).

God commands us not to worry about anything, because he is taking care of us. He advises us to pray instead of worrying. "Don't worry about anything; instead, pray about everything. Tell God what you need, and thank him for all he has done" (Philippians 4:6 NLT).

If God cares enough to supply all our basic needs—food, shelter, and clothing—then how much more do you think he will care about our emotional state and healing our wounds?

Crying Out

In situations surrounding abuse, it is easy for us to feel disconnected from God. It is easy to believe that God doesn't care about us, much less love us. We may feel like David in Psalm 142: "When I look beside me, I see that there is no one to help me, no one to protect me. No one cares for me" (Psalm 142:4 GNTD). In other words, we feel abandoned.

We may even be like the psalmist Heman, a man who knew God intimately, who called God the God of his salvation and was constantly in prayer. Even during his time of affliction, Heman prayed, "O Lord, God of my salvation, I have cried out day and night before you. Let my prayer come before you; Incline your ear to my cry" (Psalm 88:1–2 NKJV).

Have you cried out to God? "For he will deliver the needy who cry out, the afflicted who have no one to help. He will take pity on the weak and the needy and save the needy from death. He will rescue them from oppression and violence, for precious is their blood in his sight" (Psalm 72:12–14 NIV).

Believing that God sees us and cares about us requires faith. Reaching a place of acceptance and even forgiveness for your abuser will take time, but it is possible because of God's grace and effort on your part. In Jesus, there is healing and freedom. Call out to God in your distress.

Some people think prayers are supposed to be long and elaborate, telling God how much they love him. But prayers are actually just conversations with God. If you're hurt, angry, or broken, don't hold that all inside. Instead, release those feelings to the one who cares about you and wants to comfort you. Cry out to God, right this moment! Tell him exactly how you feel, and don't hold back. "O God, listen to my cry! Hear my prayer!" (Psalm 61:1 NLT).

Abandonment

When we're feeling abandoned, the Devil capitalizes on that to try and turn us into what Edward T. Welch refers to as an "Atheistic Believer," where you believe "God exists, yet you feel increasingly isolated and alone. The more extreme the suffering, the more intense is the sense of aloneness,"[5] and we may begin to doubt God's existence. And that, my dear friend, is a dangerous place to be. "My God, My God, why have you forsaken me? Why are you so far from helping Me, and from the words of my groaning?" (Psalm 22:1 NLT).

When we feel abandoned, will we trust God in the midst of our pain? Will we allow our worship to renew our minds and the way we view God? Or will we allow the Devil to tear us away from the one who knew us before forming us in the womb? "But you are holy ... they trusted, and you delivered them. They cried to you, and were delivered; they trusted in you, and were not ashamed ... But you are he who took me out of the womb; you made me trust while on my mother's breasts ... From my mother's womb you have been my God" (Psalm 22:3–5, 9–10 NKJV).

---

5 Welch, Edward T.

God promises to never abandon us, and God is a—well—a God of his word. So, if he promises to never leave us, then we can believe it. "The LORD himself goes before you and will be with you; he will never leave you nor forsake you. Do not be afraid; do not be discouraged" (Deuteronomy 31:8 NIV).

Shared Suffering

The Devil wants us to believe that our abuse occurred because God turned his back on us, and that we were forced to suffer because God's loving hand was no longer on our lives. The Devil wants us to believe that God is far away and indifferent to our sufferings. But if this were true, why would God send his only son to share in our sufferings?

God chose to send his son to become like man, his creation, and willingly suffer a horrifying death. Would a distant and indifferent God take human form and endure every type of suffering and pain imaginable? Jesus was oppressed, afflicted, despised, and rejected. The people who lined up just to touch his hand and praise him were the same people who later turned away from him to avoid seeing his face. As a sufferer, himself, Jesus recognizes and shares in our suffering. In other words, when you were abused, Jesus was abused, too. You were not alone, because Christ was right there with you.

Victory in Suffering

Would you believe me if I said there is victory in suffering? Before you call me crazy, please just read me out. Suffering accomplishes the following:

1. Suffering makes us more obedient. "Before I was afflicted I went astray, but now I keep your word" (Psalm 119:67 NKJV).

2. Suffering deepens our insight into God's vision. "It is good for me that I have been afflicted, that I may learn your statutes" (Psalm 119:71 NKJV).
3. Suffering increases our compassion and effectiveness in ministry. "Blessed be the God and Father of our Lord Jesus Christ, the Father of mercies and God of all comfort, who comforts us in all our tribulation, that we may be able to comfort those who are in any trouble, with the comfort with which we ourselves are comforted by God" (2 Corinthians 1:3–4 NKJV).
4. Suffering teaches us to wait patiently on God. "Wait on the Lord; be of good courage, and he shall strengthen your heart; wait, I say, on the Lord!" (Psalm 27:14 NKJV).
5. Suffering helps us develop a joy less dependent on our circumstances. "My lips quivered at the voice; rottenness entered my bones; and I trembled in myself, that I might rest in the day of trouble. When he comes up to the people, he will invade them with his troops. Though the fig tree may not blossom, nor fruit be on the vines; though the labor of the olive may fail, and the fields yield no food; though the flock may be cut off from the fold, and there be no herd in the stalls—yet I will rejoice in the God of my salvation. The Lord God is my strength" (Habakkuk 3:16–19 NKJV).
6. Suffering helps us appreciate God even more as he restores us. "And the Lord restored Job's losses … indeed the Lord gave Job twice as much as he had before.… Now the Lord blessed the latter days of Job more than his beginning" (Job 42:10, 12 NKJV).

It's hard to believe, but there are benefits to suffering. I can personally testify to that. Before allowing God to heal me, I allowed my suffering to be an excuse for me to live life my way. But by "doing me" I only became more miserable, lost, broken, and confused.

Allowing God into my heart to heal and make me whole has been the greatest decision I ever made.

Through my suffering, I have truly become more appreciative and knowledgeable of whom God is as he restored me. My abuse ultimately led me back to God and as he worked on my heart I developed a true relationship with him rather than the superficial one I had before. As I experienced his love I began to develop a heart of worship where all I want to do is live for and please him.

My suffering has allowed me to awaken my purpose as I have grown more compassionate toward those who have endured all types of abuse. My own abuse has caused me to become more effective in the ministry to which God has called me—to encourage, uplift, love, and heal. Through my suffering, I have developed a joy that is independent of my situation. No matter my circumstances, I am at peace because I know God will make a way.

I am in no way advocating that people should be abused just so they can reap the benefits of their suffering. But people who have been abused can find the brighter side of a dark story. Again, no pain need be suffered in vain.

The Blame Game

I understand. It's much easier to blame God for what happened to us. It's much easier to allow the shame from our abuse to keep us isolated. It is much easier to allow the voices of humiliation and condemnation to prevent us from developing an authentic relationship with God and meaningful relationships with others.

But if we decide to take the easier route, the Devil wins. Jesus allowed himself to be crucified and hung on a cross so that he could conquer death. Through his resurrection, Jesus declared that God is more powerful than the Devil, and he will *not* allow the Devil to win. God has already won the war, and he is certainly capable of winning this small battle!

Why am I so confident that through Christ you are able to win?

"But you belong to God, my dear children. You have already won a victory over those people, because the Spirit who lives in you is greater than the spirit who lives in the world" (1 John 4:4 NLT). You belong to God—and because you are a child of God, the Spirit of God lives within you.

"The Spirit of God, who raised Jesus from the dead, lives in you. And just as God raised Christ Jesus from the dead, he will give life to your mortal bodies by this same Spirit living within you" (Romans 8:11 NLT).

If you believe that Jesus was indeed raised from the dead, and if you have accepted Jesus as your personal savior, then the Spirit of God dwells within you. If you haven't, it is not too late. Actually, right now is the perfect time to accept Christ into your life and allow him to heal and lead you. Turn to the chapter titled "The Invitation" and invite God into your life.

If you have already professed belief in Christ's resurrection and invited him into your life, then the Spirit of God lives within your heart. It is this Spirit that gives you the power to defeat all attacks of the enemy, the principalities of darkness, and the evil one.

Prayer

Lord, thank you for reminding me that you are always with me. And for those times when I thought I was alone, thank you for carrying me. Lord, thank you for sharing in my suffering and, as a result of my pain, drawing me closer to you.

I invite your Holy Spirit to live within me and to give me the strength I need to defeat the enemy. I declare that no weapon formed against me will prosper.

In Jesus' name, amen.

4

WHO ARE YOU?

But you, God, see the trouble of the afflicted;
you consider their grief and take it in hand.
The victims commit themselves to you; you are
the helper of the fatherless. Break the arm of the
wicked man; call the evildoer to account for his
wickedness that would not otherwise be found out.
—Psalm 10:14–15 (NIV)

Psalm 10:14–15 describes God as being empathetic toward our pain, as a comforter to those who have been victimized, a helper to those in need, a father, and justice itself. I have personally experienced God as being all these things and more. I have felt God's love and compassion, I have experienced his healing, and I have been comforted by him. I invite you to learn who God is for yourself — and as a result, learn who you are because of him.

Who Is He?

The Bible describes God as, "The Lord, the Lord, the compassionate and gracious God, slow to anger, abounding in love and faithfulness, maintaining love to thousands, and forgiving wickedness, rebellion and sin. Yet he does not leave the guilty unpunished; he punishes the children and their children for the sin of the fathers to the third and fourth generation" (Exodus 34:6–7 NIV).

God is compassionate and gracious because he extends his love to all, even though none of us deserve it. Titus 3:5 tells us "he saved us, not because of works done by us in righteousness, but according to his own mercy, by the washing of regeneration and renewal of the Holy Spirit" (ESV). Despite how messed up we are, he offers forgiveness to those who seek him, while punishing those who choose not to. "If we confess our sins, he is faithful and just and will forgive us our sins and purify us from all unrighteousness" (1 John 1:9 NIV).

The Bible is full of promise after promise that God made and honored. After Noah, God promised never again to destroy the world by flood. God promised Abraham and Sarah that even in their old age they would have a child, and they did. God promised to send a messiah to save his people, and he sent his son to save us all. Unlike man, God does not lie, nor does he disappoint. God is perfect. "God is not a man, that he should lie, nor a son of man, that he should change his mind. Does he speak and then not act? Does he promise and not fulfill?" (Numbers 3:19 NIV).

"Surely God is my help; the Lord is the one who sustains me" (Psalms 54:4 NIV). "God is our refuge and strength, an ever-present help in trouble" (Psalm 46:1 NIV). Refuge is defined as the condition of being safe or sheltered from pursuit, danger, or trouble. God provides a firm foundation where we are safe from the storms of life. This is not to say that life will be without troubles. But in our times of need, we can count on God to provide protection, to strengthen, and to offer help.

"Come to me, all who are weary and burdened and I will give you rest" (Matthew 11:28 NIV). Jesus invites you to stop trying to survive this thing called life on your own. He is offering to help you by taking on your burdens, pain, abuse, and sorrows, and exchanging them for rest. With rest comes an intimate relationship with, and knowledge of, God. With rest comes love, forgiveness, mercy, and grace. With rest comes strength, confidence, hope, and peace. God wants you to rest in the midst of the afflictions, trials, and troubles of life, with full assurance that all things will work for your good. Are you ready to get some rest?

God and Me

Now that the Bible has revealed to you who God is, allow me to share with you who God is to me.

God is my healer. He tore off the old bandages I was using to cover up my abuse, pain, and insecurities. He exposed my lack of confidence, my poor body image, and my low self-esteem. He exposed my vulnerabilities—not to make me ashamed, but to reveal how desperately I was in need of him. He took his time dealing with each and every detail, until I was capable of looking at my past and seeing victory. Because of his healing, I am confident and I have learned how to love myself.

God is my father, husband, and best friend. Unlike man, God cannot fail or disappoint. And let's be honest—man has disappointed us. Our own family, friends, peers, coworkers, and even strangers have disappointed us. But not God! During my healing process, I chose to pursue God and completely surrender to him. I chose to be involved in an intimate relationship with him. After a bad day, I turn to him. After a good day, I turn to him. I am in constant communication with God. When I am angry, I tell him. When I am happy, I tell him. When I am confused, I ask for his guidance. His praises are continuously in my mouth.

God is love! Before my healing, I never believed in love. In my opinion, love was just a man-made ideology that people misused in order to take advantage of others. It was love that had abused me, attempted to break me, and brought me much pain. But as God healed my every deep wound, he redefined love for me. The definition he offered me was that love is God!

27

God's love for me sent his only son to be crucified on a cross. His love knew me before I was even placed in my mother's womb. His love molded and shaped me, and counted every hair on my head. God loved me even when I didn't love myself. He loved me when I thought I was unworthy and underserving of love.

God's love is unconditional. He does not love me only if I do this or that. He loves me just because—well, because he doesn't need a reason. His love is transforming, healing, and comforting. Because of God's love for me, I now understand what love truly is. I am able to offer that unconditional love to others and receive it from them as well.

Will you accept God's offer of love? "Love is patient, love is kind. It does not envy, it does not boast, it is not proud. It does not dishonor others, it is not self-seeking, it is not easily angered, it keeps no record of wrongs. Love does not delight in evil but rejoices with the truth. It always protects, always trusts, always hopes, always perseveres" (1 Corinthians 13:4–7 NIV).

The Unforgiving Servant

"The kingdom of heaven is like a certain king who wanted to settle accounts with his servants. And when he had begun to settle accounts, one was brought to him who owed him ten thousand talents. But as he was not able to pay, his master commanded that he be sold, with his wife and children and all that he had, and that payment be made. The servant therefore fell down before him, saying, 'Master, have patience with me, and I will pay you all.' Then the master of that servant was moved with compassion, released him, and forgave him the debt. But the servant went out and found one of his fellow servants who owed him a hundred denarii; and he laid hands on him and took him by the throat, saying, 'Pay me what you owe!' So his fellow servant fell down at his feet and begged him, saying 'Have patience with me, and I will pay you all.' And he would not, but went and threw him into prison till he should pay the debt. So when his fellow servants saw what had been done, they were very grieved, and came and told their master all that had been done. Then his master, after he had called him, said to him, 'You wicked servant! I forgave you all that debt because you begged me. Should you not also have had compassion on your fellow servant, just as I had pity on you?' And his master was angry, and delivered him to the torturers until he should pay all that was due to him" (Matthew 18:23–34 NKJV).

What are your thoughts after reading this story? It makes me think about how great the king was for forgiving such a large debt, how unfair the servant was toward his own peer, and how much worse off the servant ended up because he had been unable to forgive someone else.

Jesus' parables are meant to teach us, and this one is no different. In this parable, the king is God and we are the servant begging and pleading for our own forgiveness. And because God loves us, he forgives us. Selah! (Praise break!)

And then, just like the servant, we are asked to forgive our own abuser. They come begging, pleading, and apologizing—or maybe they never acknowledge what they did to us. But we have to choose whether to forgive or not.

To Forgive or Not to Forgive

Exodus 34:7 says, "He does not leave the guilty unpunished." Perhaps the person who abused you seems to be doing fine and enjoying life, whereas you are left to pick up your broken pieces. You are hurting, but they seem to be doing great. Unfair, isn't it? Not really, because God promises that the guilty will not go unpunished.

Granted, we want God to punish them right now—right this minute! Actually, we also want to witness the punishment firsthand. Maybe we imagine that it will offer us some degree of comfort, or that it will be entertaining to see our abuser hurt as much as we did. But God challenges us to literally be the bigger person and—Dare I say it?—*forgive*!

"But God, he raped me. He put his hands on me. He constantly told me that I was nothing. Why should I forgive someone who is not worthy of my forgiveness?"

Why?—because forgiveness is more for us than for our abusers. . "For if you forgive men when they sin against you, your heavenly Father will also forgive you. But if you do not forgive men their sins, your Father will not forgive your sins" (Matthew 6:14–15 NIV).

Truth be told, we all have sinned and fallen short of the glory of the Lord, so we are all in need of forgiveness. But the forgiveness of our sins depends on whether we're able to forgive others. Why should God offer forgiveness to someone who is unable to forgive someone else? Why should God show us mercy, love, and compassion if we refuse to show mercy, love, and compassion toward someone else? God commands us to "be kind and compassionate to one another, forgiving each other, just as in Christ God forgave you" (Ephesians 4:32 NIV).

If we decide to be like the unforgiven servant from the parable, we will be "delivered to the torturers." I don't know about you, but I'd rather go through the temporary pain of forgiving someone than spend eternity in hell being tortured.

Forgiving is not easy, but it is not impossible with God's help. In her article "Four Steps to Help You Genuinely Forgive," Joyce Meyer breaks forgiveness down for us:

1. Make a quality decision. Choosing to forgive is a serious decision that will not happen overnight. Forgiving someone

may be uncomfortable or even painful, but the reward is worth going through. Once you have chosen to forgive, you must be intentional in actually forgiving the person. And don't just forgive them. You must also "keep no record of wrongs," according to 1 Corinthians 13:5. When you truly forgive people, you no longer hold what they did to you against them.

2. Depend on God. Pray, ask, and depend on God to give you the strength you will need in order to forgive.

3. Understand your emotions. During this forgiving process, your emotions will need time to catch up with your decision to forgive. We are advised to not act on our feelings, because of how fickle they are. Remember why you decided to forgive.

4. Pray for your enemies. In Matthew 5:44, Jesus instructs us to love our enemies and pray for those who persecute us. Praying for the person who abused you is one of the toughest things you will ever want to do, but God tells us to do so for our own benefit.[6]

You now have a choice. By choosing to forgive, you can overcome your abuser's evil with God's good. If you do that, you'll experience a new level of joy that you didn't know was possible. I encourage you to begin the process of forgiveness, because the freedom you will experience is worth it.

I Forgave

I would not advise you to do something that I personally have not done. To complete my own healing process, God showed me that in addition to forgiving those who had abused me, I needed to forgive myself. For me, forgiving myself was the biggest challenge.

First, let me say that when you forgive, a heavy weight will be

---

[6] Meyer, Joyce.

lifted from your heart and you will experience freedom. When you choose to remain angry and bitter toward your abuser, you allow the hurt and pain to build up in your heart, which will cause you to hurt and inflict pain on others. As the saying goes, "Hurt people hurt people." Although the abuse has ended, you are still allowing that person to maintain a hold on you. You are allowing your abuser to affect your future relationships and how you interact with others by continuing to affect your emotions and behavior. While your abuser is out living his or her life, you continue to suffer.

And, my dear friend, it is time for you to stop suffering. Forgive and let go! Forgive, so that you will no longer be held captive by your abuser. Let go, so that God can finish healing you.

Just because you forgive does not mean your abuser walks away scot-free. One day, your abuser will have to answer to God and pay for what he or she has done. God says, "It is mine to avenge; I will repay. In due time their foot will slip; their day of disaster is near and their doom rushes upon them" (Deuteronomy 32:35 NIV). "Do not take revenge, my dear friends, but leave room for God's wrath, for it is written: 'It is mine to avenge; I will repay,' says the Lord" (Romans 12:19 NIV).

If you are anything like me, you may have to forgive yourself as well. I blamed myself for what happened. I believed that because I did not stop it or tell anyone, I allowed the abuse to take place. But God revealed to me how untrue that was, and that I was not to blame for the actions of someone else.

Many abused people are silenced and made to believe the abuse is their own fault, which causes them to hide in shame. But God wants me to tell you what he told me—it is not your fault! Stop believing the lies of the enemy, who wants you to feel disgusted and ashamed. There is nothing shameful about what happened to you.

So take a second and forgive yourself for blaming yourself and believing the lies of the enemy. Ask God to restore within you a healthy feeling of self-worth. Ask God to replace your shame with confidence. Ask God to show you that you are a victor—not a victim.

Prayer

Lord, forgive us our sins as we forgive those who have sinned against us. God, you know this is no easy task. I call on you to give me the strength I need to forgive the one who hurt me in unimaginable ways.

Lord, I no longer want to be held captive by the hurt and pain that person inflicted on me. I wish to experience freedom, healing, and a complete transformation. And as I let go, erase every desire for revenge from my heart. I give that person to you, Lord, because vengeance is yours.

And as I forgive that person, Lord, help me to forgive myself. Help me to stop playing victim or blaming myself. Remind me of who you are, and teach me how to love myself the same way you love me. Help me to find my worth in you and understand who I am because of you.

In Jesus' name I pray, amen.

5

CLOSING REMARKS

As we approach the end of this book, just know that this is not the end of your journey. I pray this book has helped you in more ways than I can ever imagine. I hope my story has inspired you to start rewriting your own story. Write a story that acknowledges God even in the midst of pain. Write a story of healing, strength, and victory. Write a story that declares that you are a victor and not a victim. Finally, write a story that God will use to inspire and encourage others.

I pray that your journey does not end when you close this book, but that it will continue until you have exchanged all your hurt and pain for God's rest, love, joy, and peace. I am praying for you!

Prayer

Lord, I want to thank you for this individual who read this book. I pray this book has given them the strength that they needed to not only begin but complete their journey of healing. I pray this book has encouraged them to seek you and live a life of meaning.

I pray that they become completely healed as your love pieces them together. I pray that you continue to take their pain and turn it into praise. May they no longer see themselves as a victim but as a victor. Help them to find freedom from their abuse as you give them the power to forgive and let go.

Help them to no longer be silenced by their pain but instead sing a song of praise. May they begin to stand confidently on your word and know who they are because they know who you are.

Lord, thank you for being near to us who are brokenhearted and comforting us during our time of need. Thank you for your unconditional love that not only saves but heals. Thank you for showing us that our story does not end with abuse and like Jesus we have the power to rise up from our pain and overcome our situation. Thank you for taking what the devil meant for evil and turning it around for our good.

Thank you for giving me this platform to speak to your people in need and I pray that one day they too will use their personal story of abuse to encourage someone else.

In Jesus' name I pray, Amen.

THE INVITATION

If you recognize that you are a sinner, and you desire a relationship with God, say this prayer:

> *Father, I know that I have broken your laws and my sins have separated me from you. I am truly sorry, and now I want to turn away from my past sinful life toward you. Please forgive me, and help me avoid sinning again. I believe that your son, Jesus Christ, died for my sins, was resurrected from the dead, is alive, and hears my prayer. I invite Jesus to become the Lord of my life, to rule and reign in my heart from this day forward. Please send your Holy Spirit to help me obey you, and to do your will for the rest of my life. In Jesus' name I pray, Amen.*[7]

If you decided to pray this prayer, repent of your sins, and receive Christ today, welcome to God's family!

Now, as a way to grow closer to him, the Bible tells us to follow up on our commitment. Join a local church where you can worship God and get baptized. Spend time with God each day, and develop the habit of praying daily and reading his word. Share your faith with someone, fellowship with others, and develop a group of believing friends who can support you on your journey.

---

[7] "Prayer of Salvation."

SOURCES

Meyer, Joyce. "Four Steps to Help You Genuinely Forgive." *Joyce Meyer Ministries*. *www.joycemeyer.org/articles/ea.aspx?article=four_steps_to_help_you_genuinely_forgive.*

"Prayer of Salvation." *All About God*. *www.allaboutgod.com/prayer-of-salvation.htm.*

Welch, Edward T. "When It Seems Like God Has Abandoned You." Excerpted from *Depression: A Stubborn Darkness*. Punch Press, 2004. *Family Life*. *www.familylife.com/articles/topics/life-issues/challenges/depression/when-it-seems-like-god-has-abandoned-you.*

"Why Does God Allow Evil?" *Got Questions Ministries*. *https://www.gotquestions.org/God-allow-evil.html*

Made in the USA
Middletown, DE
11 November 2017